THE HOUSE OF GHOSTS AND MIRRORS

Oz Hardwick was born in Plymouth, 1960. He is the author of five previous collections of poetry, most recently *The Ringmaster's Apprentice*, published by Valley Press in 2014. He is a Professor of Creative Writing at Leeds Trinity University, and an accomplished photographer and musician. He lives in York.

The House of Ghosts and Mirrors

Oz Hardwick

Valley Press

First published in 2017 by Valley Press
Woodend, The Crescent, Scarborough, YO11 2PW
www.valleypressuk.com

First edition, first printing (September 2017)

ISBN 978-1-908853-85-1
Cat. no. VP0102

A CIP record for this book is available from the British Library.

Cover photograph by Oz Hardwick.
*"Although the bed itself was replaced on a number of occasions, it's where I
came into the world, reflected in the same dressing-table mirror."*

Cover design by Jamie McGarry. Text design by Jo Haywood.
Edited by Martha Sprackland.

Printed and bound in Great Britain by
Imprint Digital, Upton Pyne, Exeter.

Contents

The Pros and Cons of Immortality 13

In a Glass House 14

Archaeology 15

Stars like Sentinels Stand By 16

Life Cycle 17

Devon Tin 18

Dog Star 19

Baba Yaga 20

Street of Small Windows 21

Leaves 22

A Promise of Snow 23

Doppler 24

Afterparty 25

After the Late Shift 26

Bass 27

Not So Sweet 28

Tied 29

Ophelia in Leeds 6 30

Status Update 31

Figure in the Landscape 32

The Miracle of Flight 33

Not that Sort of Hero 35

Lacuna 36

Sail 37

The Apotheosis of Ceyx 38

Small Change 39

Exchange 40

Hortus Conclusus 41

The Gift 42

The Early Train 43

The Inspector 44

The Ruins at Night 45

Mistranslation 46

Vague 47

Flying over Toronto 48

Crash 49

Patience 50

Ice 51

A Change in the Weather 52

The Return 53

October 54

Trick or Treat 55

Seance 56

Wishbones 57

Ivy 58

Knitting 59

Mothers' Day 60

Mother 61

Sleep 62

Tristan on the Midnight Road 63

In the Snow Globe 64

Mapping Space 65

Emptying the Cupboard 66

The Contract 67

The Ghost House 68

Acknowledgements

Versions of some of the poems in this collection have appeared in *Black Light Engine Room*, *The Book of Plans, Hopes & Dreams* (Beautiful Dragons), *Bridgewatcher* (SPM), *Café Review*, *CC&D*, *Corpse Roads* (Wyrd Harvest), *Dream Catcher*, *Fires in the North*, *How am I doing for Time?* (PP&P), *HQ*, *The Interpreter's House*, *Journeys* (Wordspace/IDP), *Leads to Leeds*, *The Loneliness Project* (Theatre Cloud), *Lost & Found* (Silver Birch Press), *Orbis*, *The Quality of the Moment* (Red Shed), *Reach*, *Snapping Turtle*, *Still Life with Wine & Cheese* (Stairwell), *Three Drops from a Cauldron*, *Under the Fable*, *Visual Verse*, *Winter Fires* (IDP), *Wyrd Words & Effigies*.

This volume's epigraph, 'In a Glass House' and 'Stars like Sentinels Stand By' appear on Peter Byrom-Smith & Oz Hardwick, *The House of Memory* (Debt Records, 2017), and 'Life Cycle' was written for Stefanie Elrick & Loren Fetterman's *Kairos* performance (Manchester Cornerhouse, 2015).

'Stars like Sentinels Stand By' quotes from the unpublished poem 'Ham Woods' by George H Lowden (1896-1979).

I would like to thank Martha Sprackland for her insightful editing.

This book is dedicated to all who called number 37 home
– or simply felt at home there – between 1955 and 2015.

close to the border
where mapmakers lose themselves
a house of mirrors

The Pros and Cons of Immortality

Is it really so bad to begin with an ending?

Here I am, queueing for dreams
in a new world that hardens around me
like a scab on the wound of growing apart
from where I belong, what I know.

So, I ask again, is it really so bad
to be here, where walls crumble,
where your solitary love
is long gone and, surely, forgotten?

Because from here – half a century away,
and counting – even I forget
most of the time. *But
that's what hurts*, you tell me,
the long forgetting that hangs
in the air, its cold breath
dampening your sleepless face.

You forget everything
one heartbeat at a time
until you forget yourself.
But is that really so bad?

In a Glass House

an inscription in a vicarage window

Everything looks smaller inside
as you drift from room to room,
crossing boundaries, searching
for a detail of your long imagination.
Books line the walls, obscuring
cobbled streets, slate sky,
wooden passers-by,
lines of tourists snaking
across the grass, waiting
to see their own reflections
in the dead poet's lines.
At last you find it,
perfectly small, fragile
beneath glass eaves.

The air smells familiar:
pipe tobacco, tomatoes,
paraffin, polish. Your eyes
sting with forgetfulness, until,
catching the light, you discover
a tiny imperfection, scratched
lightly at first, later more firmly –
a dead man's name.

On tumbling shelves
books remain unread.

Archaeology

When I lifted the floorboards, I found myself
face to face with my father, younger than I am now.
His sleeves were rucked up, and he bit his tongue
in concentration as he dusted himself down
with a souvenir clothes brush from Toronto,
bought when it was a small town, when my grandfather
named his village and his children. He lay,
oil under his cracked nails, ten No. 6
and a brass lighter packed in his shirt pocket,
stretched on a crucifix of chimneysweep's brushes.

He nodded to the shadows, where my girlfriend lay
dead, wound in a sari steeped in mothballs.
Don't let me catch you down here, he smiled,
but we both knew I had no choice.

Stars like Sentinels Stand By

The moon is heavy tonight,
plump and livid, barely clearing
the black ground. It eyes nothing.
Broken-toothed hills snap at its arc.
It's nights like this I feared,
swollen with superstition and ill omen,
dark mezzotints in the Family Bible.

You read it all before I was born,
in dog-eared cards and damp tealeaves,
thumbed almanacs and the turn of the sky,
your milky eyes piercing the future.

The last bite of the moon disappears,
leaving me with paper saints,
eagles, lions and lambs; guardians
you set to watch my solitary transit.

Life Cycle

We swim in silver, bloom in winter light,
shedding shells, green and gold,
breathing hard through root and branch,
cold air buoying pollen.

Cells divide to slow maturity,
gulping rain, born of water,
facing the sun, fast and fertile and
our young hearts race away,

restlessly growing, forgetting home
as we fly, pulsing into true forms,
swarming in cycles, dipping and dripping
with spent days until we fall

two thousand years, diving deep,
seeds scattering and breaking
the surface, green and gold,
streaming, blooming, swimming in silver.

Devon Tin

Sardines, coke, the Coronation.
Granddad's tobacco, Dad's
screws and washers, fuses,
baby food, Festival of Britain,
Quality Street, 3in1.
Mum's buttons. They
speak through cans linked
by miles of string.
Listen. A voice of rust,
pipe smoke, bitten tongues,
carbonated giggles, needles.
Broken biscuits, blistered fingers,
TCP. Frayed bunting, Christmas
lights, coiled wire,
paint and Jelly Babies.

Still here, as true
as the last fruit gum,
as bike-shed promises,
as the star of my cowboy childhood
warm beneath my clothes,
as the black lips calling,
the tongue already tasting
the stannary fee.

Dog Star

In the night city, astrologers conspire
at curtained windows, weighing gravity,
eyes steady on fixed points. Somewhere
between science and sleight of hand,

freed by fire and falling, white hot
in late November sky, almost unnoticed,
a prophecy grows hard edges,
warps the air, feels the draw of dirt.

We sort trinkets, mementos,
threads and trophies, airborne debris
by which we have plotted our course,
wondering where the sun will rise.

Baba Yaga

A fever night: a line where day becomes
tomorrow, a memory, an unsettling rumour –
and I am caught in searchlights, prisoner
of a war with myself, strung on the edge of sleep
like a skeleton wire-bound on a scaffold.

If I squint, shadows write in a language
close to my own, a sequence of instructions
I can't quite understand. This bed is a B-movie
on a TV channel no one watches, ignored
between the porn and the Evangelicals.

The air smells of sweat and pencil shavings,
gluing my face to the ceiling, as my fists fumble
feathers. I am dry, hard, bitter, clinging
to an ache that chews to my core, my legs stiff
but melting, as everything turns to faces.

Street of Small Windows

We lived on a street of small windows, with stone fists
clenched beneath tar. I saw them when the beasts came
snorting fire and chewing through the past.
I saw them from the same small window
from which I'd watched the boy raise his fingers,
glowing in gaslight, levitating through winter's dark.

A red-eyed prophet, burnt in some drunken war,
peeped through net curtains, while a fat devil,
moustache like Oliver Hardy's dark twin,
cursed his trembling hand and his only child.

In that nodding year a sickle wind teased snow,
cut a path for benign gods, triumphant on lighted chariots.
Children smeared small widows as they passed,
fanfares spinning fancies, hearts racing like deer
until silence returned its breathless benediction.

Beneath the street, tight fists relaxed,
freeing us all into the future, dimming lamps
in small windows, all painted shut.

Leaves

In that summer I discovered leaves,
explored their textures, drew in
their citrus, amber, indescribable
breath, like a lover sleeping close.

I clothed myself in leaves, weaving
too many shades to learn the names
of parent plants, dressed myself
in rippling green finer than light.

And I slept deep in leaves, nested
like a mouse, bird, snake,
the phoenix rising from burning leaves,
fire blazing behind summer eyes.

A Promise of Snow

She told me ice takes different shapes
when played different types of music,
that snow grows its mirror image
according to songs of the wind,
its crystal partners' fingers touching
lightly in a slow circle dance. She told me
that the Snow Queen gathers clouds
of white bees humming to the hive
at winter's heart, a palace cocooned
in glass and silver, mirrored scales.

And as she spoke, she poured wine,
white and chilled, catching light
from the crackling fire, where a cat sat
straight and staring, its back to the flames,
its eyes bright with reflected frost.

Doppler

We met on the darkest night of the year,
when the sky was tattooed with stars
that needled space to black streets.

A few snowflakes, flicked from invisible
clouds, caught in my hair and pricked
my upturned face, but didn't settle.

And as I thought of light and distance,
clear moments, millennia in the making,
a single flake caught my tongue. I found

my arms wrapped tight around a dream
of a blue shift, spun from nowhere,
from the vast, incalculable chance of time,

but scattered before my fingers closed.
There are glow stars on my ceiling, a print
on my pillow like the skeleton of a small hand.

I bend to study the charts, consider
lines and angles, calculate the distance
between void and memory,

but find nothing.
Galaxies pass
like night and snow.

Afterparty

It was a big house, a lot of land,
and I couldn't remember who'd invited me.
There were tyre tracks on the lawn and the carpet,
but the party was winding down, tangled
bodies on couches, on the landing,
in the flower beds, leaving just
a few of us, jittery with crystals and capsules.
Someone said *Read us one of your poems*
so I pulled out a couple of books and flipped
through dog-eared pages. But I didn't recognise
any of the words, and my eyes blurred
over unfamiliar phrases, and there was
an awkward, jerky silence, until
someone said *Look, are you a poet
or what?* But by then my mouth was dry
as I licked my sour, powdered finger,
leafing frantically through hazy titles
I couldn't focus on, everyone getting restless.
And all I could think of as the room spun sideways
was your smile as you'd left, hours earlier, your arm
resting lightly around someone else's waist.

After the Late Shift

after Edward Hopper's 'Automat'

She is waiting for the darkness to take shape,
to enter through the swing doors and occupy
the empty chair at the white table,
brushing warm lips on her cool nape.

She is waiting for the darkness to take shape,
smile slightly, conspiratorially. Then –
as she raises her young face, locks
unflinching eyes – she will decide.

Next, she will place her cup delicately
on the white saucer, gently remove
her left glove, and reach out.
Or perhaps she will slip on her right

and, without pause, stand up
and step into the night.
But her coffee's cold and the blinds come down
as she waits for the darkness to take shape.

Bass

These strings are antiques, dead
as bass on a slab. When I was a kid,
I'd walk through the fish market early,
and the smell still takes me back.

Our first gig was a church hall,
the summer of punk: cleared the place.
Later, we sat on the quay, Thunderbird drunk,
smoking home-grown, scrying our futures
in fish-slick ripples. Now these notes
are blunt sonar, tracking time.

We once stole a dinghy, rowed to nowhere
and back, left it like it had never gone.
Ever since, waves of *What if?* have hammered
at my shore. Tight as a hawser in a Force 8,
I finger the history of bottom E. Cast off.

If it's too loud, you're too old. Sail me back.

Not So Sweet

And every time I thought I'd got it made
It seemed the taste was not so sweet
– David Bowie, 'Changes'

There's a vampire on your staircase,
a veil woven by spiders across your eyes,
and your nails have grown to claws.

You lean close, hair brushing my thighs
as you offer jasmine tea, black paint
dripping like blood through floorboards.

Outside, seagulls tease traffic lights,
lovers meet at bus stops, cats curl,
apples drop in neglected gardens.

Your walls are papered with idols,
slick, sepia and knowing; your hearth
is a dark cave, your bed is untidy.

I watch you, barefoot in the kitchen,
tearing the flesh from tangerines,
cheeks damp with anything but tears.

Later, you turn the record over, smile
like a matinee vamp, and remember
the starving DJ chained in the cellar.

Tied

Beyond the frame hang dark birds,
pendulous and ungainly, slapping shadows
on the bleak beach. You choose to ignore
their strangled calls, though can't block out
the outlines of your name, so you cover your ears,

cover your eyes, cover the evening
with the rough scarf that bound your ankles
in the kitchen of a house that once was a church
and, before that, a desert, a forest,
a burning plain where you imagined angels

or devils, disguising themselves as birds,
ragged-winged and strutting, leaving
barbed wire patterns in the sand
sharp as the scar you hide from your mother,
that you touch when it's dark and you're all alone.

Ophelia in Leeds 6

At the wrong time, in the wrong place,
she wanted to be Ophelia,
wore Pre-Raphaelite dresses in the wrong decade,
and plucked Victorian poets from market junk.

She haunted arcades,
a castle in her head,
a gold ring to protect her
from the storm already raging.

I think of her, but can't go back –
my thoughts are still too green
to fully break – and I guess
her house will be student flats,
or gone altogether, just grass and litter.

I see her as she climbs the stairs
to an attic room with chaste ice
across the glass where she makes up
her face, her past, and countless futures
with pale men who call her mad
or don't call at all

until, on a night like any other,
her Gothic fancy takes her wrist
and draws her through the speckled mirror.

Status Update

I'm being followed by a dead girl.
When she asked to be Facebook friends
she didn't say she was dead –
it wasn't in her 'likes'
or on her timeline. Her profile
looked – looks – alive.

Each time I see her
I want her eyes not to look away,
want her to turn to look at me.
She never posts updates,
but each year I'm reminded
of her birthday.

Figure in the Landscape

I see you shortly after dawn,
your shadow
scratched upon ripe fields
the colour of old paper,
inking lines in soft light.

Your still, taut limbs
become bole and branches.
Memory makes statues of us all.

The Miracle of Flight

for Harold Walker

As a child I always wanted to fly.
Air displays thrilled me,
promised a future of wings and winds
above the earth's arc, freedom
from petty gravity.

In my grandparents' room I studied
scrapbooks – you as a young man,
clear-eyed, looking to the sky
and to a future you never saw.

Too young to understand, I held your wings,
envied you the clouds, your easy confidence
in shaky crates, flying over a foreign landscape
I had yet to see, but would come to love.

I still have your photograph, your scorched diploma,
a letter from the palace. I think of you on this short hop
to Brussels that I almost take for granted – see
an open cockpit, a young man falling from the sky
like a comet to lie, unmarked, in Belgian soil.

Then I imagine you here, sitting beside me.
You tell how it felt to challenge the sky; the noise,
the adrenaline and cold air stealing
your breath, the broad grin
of knowing yourself alive.

We toast each other with complimentary beers,
share stories about your sister – my grandmother –
and then fall silent, both in the aerial moment
we dreamed of as boys, looking down
on the peaceful fields spread out below.

Not that Sort of Hero

It was the end of a holiday,
mid-Channel on a bland ferry,
when Dad said, *it must be somewhere here*
that we were sunk. And that was it,
though there were medals he never spoke of,
photos in the chest of drawers,
and commendations in brown envelopes
that no one saw until he passed away.

He wasn't that sort of hero. He worked
from nine to five for decades, loved
his home, his family, a job well done,
a silly joke, a marching band, the sun.
He gave up smoking after fifty years,
couldn't sing (though sometimes did),
and was warm, but reserved.
I only ever saw him drunk once.

So when the Arctic Star came, seventy years late,
I could hardly equate
the hardship and fear of the polar convoy
with that small man pushing a century,
saw only instead his frozen hands
building a snowman in the winter of '63.

Lacuna

It was after the war, or perhaps in its final days;
I was young and don't remember clearly,
just a house amongst ruins, more felt than seen.

There was a bomb in the cellar, cold and silent –
nothing like the cartoons, with a sparkler fuse
or a clock to stop at the last crazy minute.

We didn't go down there, fear and dust sealing
the flimsy door, and the government sent a leaflet,
which we lost, detailing emergency procedures.

At 11am each Monday they tested the sirens,
my mother tensing at their revenant howl,
their reminders of past raids. We got on with life.

But at night I'd lie sleepless, imagining that beast
beneath the thin skin of floorboards, dozing,
fat as a whale, its pinprick eyes slightly open.

Sail

The diving boards are gone from the rocks,
the chained raft is loose and lost,
but the same waves lick the day into shape.

Though my eyes are closed, I know
my skin's the shade of candyfloss,
the breeze teasing years away

to days of arcades and Ferris wheels,
spinning high and kissing strangers
because I could, building lighthouses

of sand and aspiration to see
beyond the smudged horizon,
so far that I see myself

now. Thoughts are origami boats
folded from teen mags, pin-ups,
lipstick messages in drained bottles,

with ice cream sails that billow
like swirled cotton skirts, dancing
with dazzled gulls on a summer pier.

There's no shadow in the light that flickers
on closed eyelids; no threat
in the whispered promise of the endless sea.

The Apotheosis of Ceyx

There are rows of knitters, knitting,
sitting upon the shore, bright shawls
tight around their shoulders, clicking
their needles and tongues. They stretch
as far as the eye can see, the smooth sea
licking at their neat booties as they sit,
stately, knitting in the sun.

Now here comes one, a likely lad,
with bright blue braces, waxed moustache,
bolt upright on a baker's bike,
like a vision from a different time.
His basket bursts with brown paper bags,
ginger-strung to a toppling tower,
and he smiles as he doffs his flat black cap
to the lines of ladies, who all wave back
with smiles of their own, flushing like berries
as they watch the young man speed on
toward the jetty, where he doesn't stop,
but flies into the waves. They wave again
with their wrinkled hands, bury their faces
deep in the sand, and the tide comes in
over their heads. Their shawls transform
into gulls that circle, calling their love
from above the shore as, down in the deep,
they spy the bones of a bike, a floating cap.

Small Change

My keys and my guilt rattle in my pockets. It's a comfort
to know they're there, though I confess that I've long forgotten
what some of them are for. Sometimes they spur my skin,
an uncomfortable reminder of their presence. Other times
I look for them and can't find them. I know they're there
but can't put my hands on them. I get flustered and begin to
    panic.

My credit cards and my insecurities I keep hidden.
Wherever I am, I know I can rely on them
to maintain a steady value. They're transferable,
recognised all over the world. They look insignificant
but count for so much. I've memorised their details
yet still fear someone will steal my identity.

My diary and my regrets lie close to my heart. I'd be lost
without their neat prompts and reminders. I'm so busy
but, should I forget anything, they're there
with everything highlighted and underlined. Instantly
I recall the exact date and time, the place,
the names of everyone involved, even the things I've missed.

Exchange

A Breton evening, first time away from home,
in leather jackets and bodies that didn't fit yet,
confusion in our veins, we drank deep
on cheap cider from the hypermarket.

Schoolkids off the leash, three French words
between us, all pronounced wrong,
we smoked and shrugged with the local youths,
spoke in gestures, joked with raised eyebrows.

And how it happened, I don't recall,
but there I am, forty years younger,
kissing the quiet girl with the dark eyes
and a name I still can't spell. Now,

in the tobacco glow of streetlamps,
lost in lanes of cafés and dark churches,
I find myself asking strangers for directions,
my awkward mouth remembering her foreign tongue.

Hortus Conclusus

The coldest August of the century,
and trellises bulge damp with blown fuchsias.

We speak of our usual subjects: poetry, time,
distance. Almost touching, I am afraid

to look you in the eye. A poor would-be suitor,
I cannot sing, nor did I bring lute or psaltery.

More Man in Black than Orpheo, you know
I do not offer courtly metaphor or coarse euphemism,

yet your garden remains closed. But stop
just there. Slowly, my world tilts upside down –
I reach, and gently lift a spider from your hair.

The Gift

We met on a bridge in the shade of tall buildings.
I recall no details but his neat black suit
and discreet manner, like a high-class waiter,
a faint smell of soap and wet towels.

He passed me a small, scuffed attaché case,
spoke a few words in Italian that I didn't understand,
and we walked, shoulder to shoulder, awkward strangers,
before he vanished into an anonymous side-street.

As I headed to the hotel, I noticed cracks in the pavement
as, all around, the water continued to rise.
I climbed the stairs to my room, left the lights off,
rested the case on the bed and flipped the catch.

Inside was a small garden, with bonsai trees,
a mirror lake, manicured grass. Birds
swooped low, skittered at their reflections.
I leaned my head in close, listened to their songs.

The Early Train

I came round counting sleepers,
deep in railway dreams, stalled
in a station where stick-thin gentlemen
with frost-fringed whiskers and waistcoats
neatly braided with sugar and steel
crook their fingers, tap the glass
of golden fobs on iron chains
that bound the globe.

A million hands
haul hard, take the strain,
and the clockwork city rises, shines
like golden owls staring down empires.
Glass pavements prism light
that's split by horses and hard wheels
clattering the illustrious dead to life.

And in the roar Victoria grins,
gathers her skirts like yesterday's washing,
skips to Woodhouse Moor, laughing
and dancing like a top whipped crazy;
off the rails, amused as hell,
confounding clocks and railway time,
calling the sleepers to wake.

The Inspector

Down the aisle, a man with a sharp hat and sinkhole eyes
shuffles behind a black dog that sniffs without curiosity,
its streaked tongue lolling like a discredited flag.

This train has run so long it has worn through rails,
through sleepers, and deep into the earth, its windows smudged
with the strata of abandoned life. We sit, side by side,

alone in headphones, dry eyes flicking at screens,
searching for signals, catching announcements too late
to snatch their meanings. Stations have no names, and doors

don't open. Food was promised hours ago but
there has been no sign except the smell of bacon
or some other scorched flesh.

Down the aisle the black dog glances up,
accusing, while the inspector shuffles on,
drawing closer.

The Ruins at Night

In the ruins at night, rust remembers
the touch of hands, the play of light
on faces and bright fabrics, the quiver
of plucked strings sounding clear,
voices beneath high, arched rafters.

Dogs drink from mercury pools,
forget their masters, lick the bones
of refugees and lovers, sniff
at the intruder moon, chasing cracks
through the cradling stones.

Mistranslation

It may be a sigh; I don't remember
grief's language, its conjugations
losing me at their endings.

It may be a veil to hide the eyes
of an apiarist in his deep-sea inventory
of bees swimming through thick air.

It may be a book, or a sarcophagus
strewn with roses, blood on thorns
from thumbs that have stained pages.

And you may say it's easy, because it is,
to colour within the lines, suggest conclusions,
and seal mouths shut where hands are hidden.

Vague

Paris in grey. Your eyes, black
with secrets, suck light from morning
cafés. Lamps haze the riverside,
the news-seller blows on his cold hands,
and I dodge a 2cv, tired
flowers trailing in my sweating palm.

Jump cut: close-up, stumbling
improvisations, words
not caught, or misunderstood,
in-jokes lost between cool
jukebox tunes as I flick ash
into an empty cup and you look away.

This is the story. You may be
married, I may be wanted
for an accidental crime, but
either way we're amateurs,
and we find ourselves, awkward,
in a white apartment, sharing
smoke and philosophy. There's a gun
on the bedside table, postcards
tacked to the wall. We talk about movies
and wait for the credits to roll.

Flying over Toronto

I'm still surprised by metal in the air.
I read the science, but it made no sense,
like sound from grooved vinyl, or photographs
from whiteness in vinegary darkrooms.

At 38,000 feet I feel no pull
to the cloud-spattered ground,
yet seem to hear my father's voice, see
a childhood caught in sepia prints.

The Skylon Tower pins borrowed memories,
fingers its shadow to a girl and a boy
sitting on a step in the last century,
a fiddle playing out of frame.

And there is my father's house, long gone,
built upon, disappearing in cloud.

Crash

'Tomorrow, when resurrection comes,
The heart that is not in love will fail the test.'
– Rumi, Thief of Sleep, *trans. Shahram Shiva*

and it could have been a building that collapsed
in an earthquake far worse than the one that woke us,
confused, in the small hours, spun cobweb cracks
across the stained-glass Last Days, and made us laugh
at the prospect of the dead rising from their graves

or it could have been a car that crashed,
far worse than when, engrossed in conversation
and night, I turned right at the wrong time and smashed
into Sunday morning, where I sat in a curtained booth
afraid to raise my face towards the mirror

but I remember a black ache, edges,
your voice trembling the blistered dark

Patience

The morning angles, shuffling too much sky,
tumbling, tricking day into light: a magic lantern

slipping in and out of focus; now blade-sharp,
now soft as a slow inhale, sizing up options

on a deserted street. Doors, swollen with damp,
burst open to thumbed decks, flipping faces

familiar from a childhood lived in libraries. Glass and silver,
a heron turns, its gambler's gaze weighing

brass-bright pheasants that stud baize fields
where the day deals its shaved pack, all jokers.

Ice

It's something as simple as a January night,
hands deep in pockets, and wool
tight against your chin, echoes
of your steps marking years,
as your unthinking feet remember
shortcut lanes to old homes.

Then it's over the bridge, barely a stride
across the beck, past the bland pub –
now boarded up – that you only visited
once, in that darkest of all winters,
with friends who gathered for the final time;
and you woke next day, surprised
by the perfect clarity of the morning and your mind.

And the ice winter air tastes
of a drunken New Year's kiss
that never ended, and remains, still,
the most honest thing you ever did.

A Change in the Weather

Framed through a cracked window, the day's freeze-
frame blushes, red-sky over dry grass.
Crows stride beside rivers, geese pass
low, as the air shivers to a cat's sneeze.

Cows lie flat. Pinecones lock tight
against the angry buzz of flies scattering
beneath clouds like mirrored mountains, flattering
both moon and rising sun with halos of light.

And in countries I'll never visit, trees fall,
ice melts on tongues that trip the polygraph,
while 'mermaids' tears' sting eyes,
and small lies swell to storms, tear in half
meaningless treaties as blank
hyetographs burn.

The Return

He left some time ago, whistling tunes
that only he knew. He said they were old,
traditional Scottish, but they were different every time.

I came in from the cinema – a first date
that never showed up. I think we may have spoken,
but can't be sure. He left before breakfast.

I think I half heard him in semi-sleep,
a muffled movement downstairs.
I think perhaps he looked into my room.

I waited for him in the evening, sat in his chair,
polishing the brass firedogs, whistling the tunes
I didn't think I remembered, stirring embers.

He left thirty years ago, maybe more.
Sometimes in the firelight, reflected dimly
in dusty brass, I see a familiar face.

Here he is.

October

A pumpkin – no, a turnip – leers on the stairs,
eyes glowing, square teeth set in a grin. I'm scared
to pass by the bathroom, so walk barefoot
to the outside toilet, with its scent of October
and coarse, medicated paper. There's no light,
and I feel the cold on my thin arms.

I know this space like I know my own hands;
the shelf of bottles and webs above my head,
the yard brush to my right, the wooden panel
with words too worn to read beyond my reach,
screwed upside-down to the door. It's a refuge,
a nest, a womb; a safe, dark space with no one
but myself and my calmed imagination.

I unbolt the door to a lynch mob of faces,
crudely carved and crawling forward, pouring
over the garden wall, bursting through the gate
and out of every drain, rank upon rank,
reeking of melting plastic, scorched turnip –
no, pumpkin – and blackening flesh.

Trick or Treat

She lived in the chill whisper of an empty house,
in shapes glimpsed through midnight windows.

As children at Halloween, we'd wait, bold and bragging,
at the foot of her steps, until our laughter choked like dust
in our throats, and we ran, blind, to the safety of home fires.

Thirty years on I see her eyes in darkness,
my heart still running from rags and feathers.

Seance

We tap the table, our hands in plain sight,
no hidden tricks and wires to spell the messages

forming between us. This trembling glass is
an invisible kiss, the friction between Russian dolls,

static between the fine hairs on our forearms.
Something takes shape in the candlelit air.

Wishbones

She lays out wishbones, boiled and polished,
or painted gold with leaf-green ribbons
at each empty sitting. Soon they will snap
like twigs, like innocence, teaching the power
of will, and dominion over bird and beast,
a feast for winter.

Upstairs, the tooth fairy,
black-mouthed at the window, sucks dreams
scented with violets and mothballs from a room
bare of all but stripped beds and damp pillowcases.

And outside, splints pitch from coarse loam,
catching pale moonlight.
Sleep, little one, sleep. The night is big and lonely,
your garden's growing pale.

Ivy

Lately she has felt the urge
to do something irresponsible,
like revisit that summer resort,
fill her pockets with fine sand
and throw it streaming from taxi windows.

Instead she remains,
her pockets heavy with keys,
watching the ivy that insinuates itself
into her brickwork, into her cupboards,
into her apologies.

Knitting

A grey woman, who should be sitting in a rocking chair,
sits instead on a straight-backed stool, her eyes closed,
knitting a scarf in yellow and blue, my first school colours.

I sit on the floor, watching as it grows, listening
to the click of the needles, and the tick of a clock
echoing from an empty room at the front of the house.

She knits fast, but the scarf grows faster, billowing
at her feet, crawling higher like morning mist
until it drapes my shoulders, caresses my throat.

Faster it grows, probing my mouth, snaking inside,
down to my guts, warming my belly, then nudging up
into my head, implacably pushing from my ears and nose.

There's a tickle growing behind my eyes before
it slips under my prickling lids. The needles now move
on their own, the stool stands vacant. I turn to the window:

the last thing I see is the woman, framed in a small yard,
her eyes still closed, her face raised to the sun, flapping
her floral apron, casting crumbs or seeds to crows.

Mothers' Day

The town is thronged with men whose hands
are unfamiliar with flowers.
The red and gold stigmata, undesired,
undeserved, are a martyrdom standing out
on a grey Sunday, the sweet perfume of sanctity
mingling with Lynx and sweat. In nearby rooms
mothers await the devotional, the kiss of peace,
the annual communion of chocolates and tea.

Against this procession, I bear your braids,
shorn at nineteen and stored in a chest
with tissue and mothballs, limp across my arms
like Bartholomew's flayed skin.

Mother

It was the last story:

dust to dust from days on end,
bottled sound in boiling rooms,
we gazed from many windows,
strangers with the same father.

Still dark outside, small sighs
lost within the larger, handicapped
by a desperate fear, I turned
to see if I might chance on answers.

Ashes to ashes: she stepped outside.

Sleep

after Max Richter

It's like slipping between sheets of ice on beds
around which nurses carry trays of starfish.
We are windmills turning underwater, petrified
forests, sails shuffling black light
in submarine theatres.

Shoals of silver clouds billow,
ropes of barnacled moonlight trail lost time.

These sharp memories
are chains drawing boats,
empty but for shadows stacked in rows.

And there is my father in the uniform
I never saw him wear, ice on his epaulettes,
watching the compass needle spin like a clock.
Fish follow, miming silent films on Saturday mornings,
and I wonder if I will ever dream again.

Tristan on the Midnight Road

I slipped away, guided by the gull-eye moon,
navigating lanes banked with guano.
We'd drunk too much, gulped potions,
a backstreet Tristan and Iseult.

We didn't spend or gamble our days,
just flung them from the cliffs,
our eyes locked tight on each other,
stretching like shadows on a broken sundial.

We swam deep in each other, swallowed
our hopes, ourselves, washed ashore married
to others, traded sea for cities, towers, castles in clouds
of exhaust fumes, cigarette smoke, stifling rooms.

The road is dark, the windscreen smeared by gulls
and rain like your voice in a shell. I am drawn
by the magnetic sea. I'm coming home,
my poison love: which sail should I raise?

In the Snow Globe

Nose to the glass, looking in, it's cold,
freezing, colder than we get at home.

Horse hooves hammer at slick streets
as carriages bundle tourists by brittle canals.

It's a hectic Age of loose painters and purse-strings,
swallowed by silt and spat out whole

to lie in the wrong century.
I stand on a bridge too short to lead me anywhere,

shuffling memories and views like tarot cards,
their faces worn blank by dead thumbs.

I deal a pattern from the past, reveal
familiar streets that are never the same twice.

Following in my own footsteps, I lose myself.
It's cold, nose to the glass, looking out.

Mapping Space

Old photographs are constellations, discrete patterns
in space. This one I have named Equus:
seven monochrome snaps of a Dartmoor pony,
my parents, my aunt, me aged maybe 2,
rising on the summer horizon. I trace their pattern
through imprecise cartography, degrees worn blank
on a hand-me-down astrolabe I learnt to read
from Chaucer, guiding my fingers through
the *umbra versa*, the Cercle of the Dayes.

Gestures appear young and easy,
but there are no reactions from these neutrons,
white dwarfs, black holes. These shapes map
my first memory, and in the years between,
light has travelled 3,233,174,989,935 miles.

Emptying the Cupboard

At the bottom of the cupboard my father built
is the lino I'd forgotten, as cold to my touch
as a winter morning, dressing for school, rushing,
three stairs at a time, to the two-bar fire, the wireless,
the settee with the slack springs. Squared like a game,
it's where I played with cars and soldiers and, later,
guitars and girls, fumbling teenage songs, rehearsing
grown-up roles I still can't play convincingly.

Splatter-patterned, in sickness I joined dots,
formed twisted faces that chased me deep beneath
nylon sheets that sparked with static as I read,
cocooned in torchlight, lost in a multiverse mapped
in that same Cartesian grid. Lost beneath school bags,
toys, then music mags, I don't even remember forgetting
such insignificant detail. But now, at the bottom
of an empty cupboard, I find everything I've lost.

The Contract

The man at the door had lips stapled shut,
a forced metallic smile like a 50s MG grille.
He had pleading eyes and a black briefcase
that begged to be held: *Take me in your arms*,
it said, *nurture me as your own*. And I did,
feeding it attics and cupboards under the stairs,
the mulch of damp plaster. It grew no larger,
but opened like a leather flower
until bees filled the house, stinging, crushing
their bodies against windows
that had not seen light for months.

It became untenable. I packed
cardboard crates with photographs and guns.
The briefcase withered to corroded clasps and hinges.

The man was still on the step, slouched
among soured milk bottles. He raised
his drawn face, his eyes blank, lips scabbed
where the staples had rusted away. He held
a piece of paper. *Sign here*, he said.

The Ghost House

I was born in the Ghost House, in the front bedroom,
at the mirror where I saw my red eyes. I screamed
in the Ghost House – a slapped baby scream
that clawed my throat – then hunkered between
stiff sheets and sighing eiderdowns.

Then I built on the Ghost House, took pills
in the Ghost House to keep me strong,
and slept when the sky was too loud.

Now I'm lost in the Ghost House, in rooms
full of exits, where all records are removed.

And in the Ghost House all that remains
loses its shape, dust sheets flutter, and candles
snuff out in a breath, like a birthday cake.